BLAZERS

WEAPONS OF WAR

WEAPONS OF ANCIENT TIMES

by Matt Doeden

Reading Consultant:
Barbara J. Fox
Reading Specialist
North Carolina State University

Content Consultant:
John C. Hendrickson
Adjunct History Professor
Minnesota State University, Mankato

Capstone
press®

Mankato, Minnesota

Blazers is published by Capstone Press,
151 Good Counsel Drive, P.O. Box 669, Mankato, Minnesota 56002.
www.capstonepress.com

Library of Congress Cataloging-in-Publication Data
Doeden, Matt.
   Weapons of ancient times / by Matt Doeden.
   p. cm. — (Blazers. Weapons of war)
   Includes bibliographical references and index.
   Summary: "Describes the weapons used in battles by ancient cultures, from
primitive weapons like stone axes to more advanced weapons such as chariots
and iron swords" — Provided by publisher.
   ISBN-13: 978-1-4296-1967-7 (hardcover)
   ISBN-10: 1-4296-1967-8 (hardcover)
   1. Military weapons — History — To 1500 — Juvenile literature.
2. Civilization, Ancient — Juvenile literature. I. Title. II. Series.
U805.D73 2009
623.4'41 — dc22   2008001987

Editorial Credits
Carrie A. Braulick, editor; Alison Thiele, designer;
   Kyle Grenz, production designer; Jo Miller, photo researcher

Photo Credits
Alamy/ilian studio, cover (bottom), 26, 29 (scale mail); Alamy/Images of
Africa Photobank, 10 (bottom), 17 (boomerangs); Alamy/The Natural
History Museum, 9 (left), 16 (wooden spear); Alamy/North Wind Picture
Archives, 7; Alamy/Stuart Abraham, 9 (right), 16 (flint stone); Art Resource,
N.Y./British Museum, 14, 17 (iron ax head); Art Resource, N.Y./Erich
Lessing, 15, 17 (iron arrowheads); Corbis/Archivo Iconografico, S.A., 13
(all), 17 (bronze arrowheads, bronze ax heads); Corbis/The Art Archive,
29 (Roman armor); Corbis/Bettmann, 20; Corbis/Werner Forman, 28
(rectangular bronze shield); Getty Images Inc./The Bridgeman Art Library/
Bronze Age, 27, 28 (round bronze shield); Getty Images Inc./The Bridgeman
Art Library/Neolithic, 10 (top), 16 (stone ax head, stone dagger); Getty
Images Inc./The Bridgeman Art Library/Prehistoric, 12, 17 (copper daggers);
Getty Images Inc./The Bridgeman Art Library/Ron Embleton, 6; Getty
Images Inc./DEA Picture Library, 5; Getty Images Inc./Dorling Kindersley,
cover (top left), 16 (flint stone dagger); Getty Images Inc./Hulton Archives/
Archive Photos, 19 (top); Getty Images Inc./Time Life Pictures/Mansell,
23; The Image Works/Alinari Archives, 29 (shin guards); The Image Works/
Topham, 29 (helmet); Mary Evans Picture Library, 11; Shutterstock/
Goydenko Tatiana, 25, 29 (Great Wall of China); Shutterstock/Marilyn Volan
(grunge background elements), all; SuperStock, Inc, cover (top right), 19
(bottom), 28 (helmet)

1 2 3 4 5 6 13 12 11 10 09 08

TABLE OF CONTENTS

WEAPONS FROM NATURE

When you think of weapons, huge bombs and speeding bullets probably come to mind. But people in ancient times had much simpler weapons.

WEAPON FACT

People living in ancient times lived more than 2,000 years ago. All years in ancient times have the letters "BC" behind them.

At first, people used weapons to hunt animals. Over time, people turned their hunting tools against one another. Weapons meant power. And every ancient army wanted all the power it could get.

THE FIRST WEAPONS

The first weapons were simple. People threw rocks. They used animal bones as clubs. Pointed sticks made deadly spears. Sharpened stones made plain daggers.

dagger — a short knifelike weapon with a sharpened surface on both sides

stone dagger with handle

boomerang

Weapons improved in the Stone Age, which ended about 10,000 years ago. People added handles to stone daggers. Wooden bows shot deadly arrows. Boomerangs zipped through the air.

boomerang — a curved stick that spins and turns in flight; some boomerangs are made to return to the thrower.

Metal weapons were a dream come true for warriors. By 5000 BC, copper knives, spear tips, and axes were proving their strength. Later, people made **bronze** weapons, which were even stronger.

bronze — a metal made of copper and tin that has a gold-brown color

bronze sword

bronze ax heads

bronze arrowheads

13

iron ax head

But even the strength of bronze didn't keep warriors satisfied. About 3,500 years ago, they charged into battle with iron weapons. Iron could be shaped easier than bronze.

iron arrowheads

HANDHELD WEAPONS

wooden spear

flint stone

stone dagger

polished stone ax head

flint stone dagger

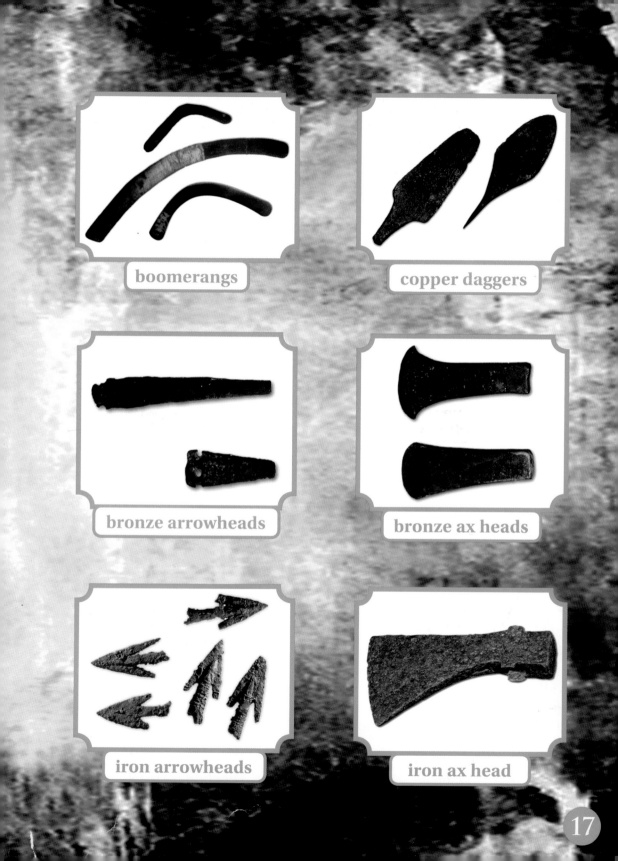

boomerangs

copper daggers

bronze arrowheads

bronze ax heads

iron arrowheads

iron ax head

BIGGER AND BETTER

Horses pulling chariots scattered enemies in a flash. Later, fighters climbed onto horses' backs. These fighters formed the first cavalries.

chariot — a wheeled fighting platform; oxen pulled the first chariots, while horses pulled later ones.

cavalry — part of an army that fights on horseback

chariot

WEAPON FACT

Soldiers in India rode elephants into battle!

catapult

People often built walls around their villages for protection. But the walls couldn't stand up to catapults. These throwing machines sent giant rocks crashing into the walls.

WEAPON FACT

Roman catapults shot 60-pound (27-kilogram) rocks more than 500 feet (152 meters).

Egyptians and Greeks built giant wooden warships. They chased down enemy ships to smash holes in them.

WEAPON FACT

Many ships could be easily taken apart and put back together. This was helpful if the warriors had to cross land.

DEFENSES

As weapons improved, defenses did too. Tall, thick stone walls protected castles, forts, and cities. The Great Wall of China protected the country's northern end.

castle — a large building where a ruler lived

WEAPON FACT

The Chinese added to the Great Wall
until the mid-1600s. Most of the wall
from ancient times has crumbled.

Fighters used strong **armor** and shields for protection. Scale mail was made of many small metal scales. Chain mail was made of metal links or rings.

armor — a protective covering worn by warriors during battle; armor was often made of metal or leather in ancient times.

scale mail

bronze shield

Weapons of ancient times were no match for today's guns and bombs. But ancient weapons were still deadly. A fighter's courage, shield, and armor were often all the protection he had.

DEFENSES

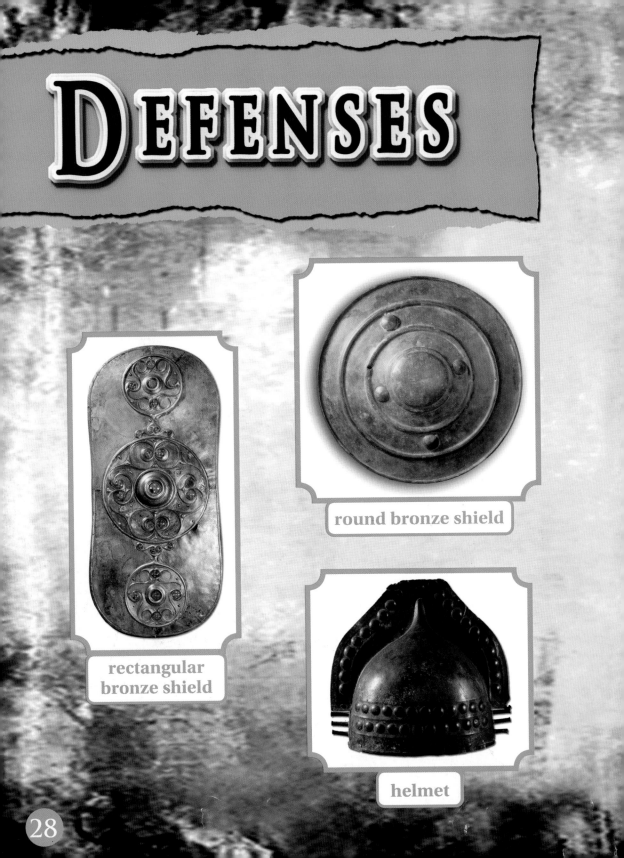

round bronze shield

rectangular
bronze shield

helmet

helmet with face shield

shin guards

Roman armor

scale mail

Great Wall of China

GLOSSARY

armor (AR-muhr) — a protective covering worn by warriors during battle

boomerang (BOO-muh-rang) — a curved stick that spins and turns in flight; some boomerangs are made to return to the thrower.

bronze (BRAHNZ) — a metal made of copper and tin; bronze has a gold-brown color.

castle (KASS-uhl) — a large, heavily protected building where a ruler lived in ancient times

cavalry (KAV-uhl-ree) — a unit of soldiers who fight on horseback

chariot (CHAYR-ee-uht) — a two-wheeled fighting platform used in ancient times that was usually pulled by a horse

dagger (DAG-ur) — a short knifelike weapon with a sharpened surface on both sides

fort (FORT) — a walled and heavily defended military base

READ MORE

Byam, Michele. *Arms and Armor.* Eyewitness Books. New York: DK, 2004.

Herbst, Judith. *The History of Weapons.* Major Inventions Through History. Minneapolis: Twenty-First Century Books, 2006.

Parks, Peggy J. *Weapons.* Yesterday and Today. San Diego: Blackbirch Press, 2005.

INTERNET SITES

FactHound offers a safe, fun way to find Internet sites related to this book. All of the sites on FactHound have been researched by our staff.

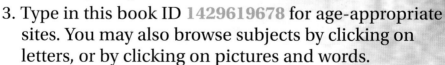

Here's how:
1. Visit *www.facthound.com*
2. Choose your grade level.
3. Type in this book ID 1429619678 for age-appropriate sites. You may also browse subjects by clicking on letters, or by clicking on pictures and words.
4. Click on the Fetch It button.

FactHound will fetch the best sites for you!

Index